LIFE SCIENCE

ADAPTATIONS

Christina Earley

A Stingray Book

Teaching Tips for Caregivers and Teachers:

This Hi-Lo book features high-interest subject matter that will appeal to all readers in intermediate and middle school grades. It may be enjoyed by students reading at or above grade level as well as by those who are looking for age-appropriate themes matched with a less challenging reading level. Hi-Lo books are ideal for ELL readers, too.

Each book appeals to a striving reader's age and maturity level. Opportunities are provided for students to read words they already know while encountering a limited number of new, high-interest vocabulary words. With these supports in place, students will read more fluently while increasing reading comprehension. Use the following suggestions to help students grow as readers.

- Encourage the student to read independently at home.
- Encourage the student to practice reading aloud.
- Encourage activities that require reading.
- Establish a regular reading time.
- Have the student write questions about what they read.

Teaching Tips for Teachers:

Before Reading

- Ask, "What do I know about this topic?"
- Ask, "What do I want to learn about this topic?"

During Reading

- Ask, "What is the author trying to teach me?"
- Ask, "How is this like something I already know?"

After Reading

- Discuss how the text features (headings, index, etc.) help with understanding the topic.
- Ask, "What interesting or fun fact did you learn?"

TABLE OF CONTENTS

WHAT ARE ADAPTATIONS?

Plants and animals have ways to survive in their **environments**.

They develop **traits** called *adaptations*.

Animals use parts of their bodies, or they take actions.

Plants also have special ways to stay alive in their surroundings.

FUN FACTS

Penguins must be excellent swimmers to hunt for food in the water.

FUN FACTS

The harpy eagle has claws about the same size as a grizzly bear's.

PHYSICAL ADAPTATIONS OF ANIMALS

Physical adaptations are the special body parts that an animal uses.

Hummingbirds use long, skinny beaks to get nectar.

Polar bears have thick fur to stay warm.

The long neck of a giraffe allows it to eat the leaves on tall trees.

BEHAVIORAL ADAPTATIONS OF ANIMALS

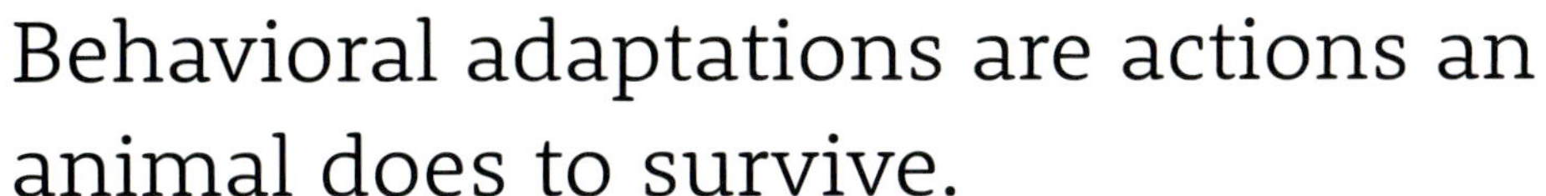

Behavioral adaptations are actions an animal does to survive.

Geese fly south in the fall to leave the cold and find food.

When they are threatened, **opossums** roll onto their backs, slow their breathing, and become stiff.

FUN FACTS

Sand snakes move sideways across hot sand.

PHYSIOLOGICAL ADAPTATIONS OF ANIMALS

Physiological adaptations are changes to the **metabolism** of an animal.

A snake makes **venom** to protect itself from **predators**.

Fish in the Arctic and Antarctic have **antifreeze** that keeps them from becoming frozen.

Many animals hibernate during the winter.

PLANTS IN THE DESERT

The **desert** is very dry.

Plants have small leaves with thick skins that hold water for a long time.

Some roots are close to the surface to get rain before it dries up.

A cactus can make more plants by breaking off pieces.

FUN FACTS

Roots can grow over 80 feet (24 meters) long to reach water that is deep underground.

PLANTS IN THE TROPICAL RAINFOREST

The tropical **rainforest** is hot with heavy rains.

Leaves have tips that drip extra water.

Roots support plants in thin soil.

Many plants are poisonous to survive being eaten by animals.

castor bean
yellow oleander

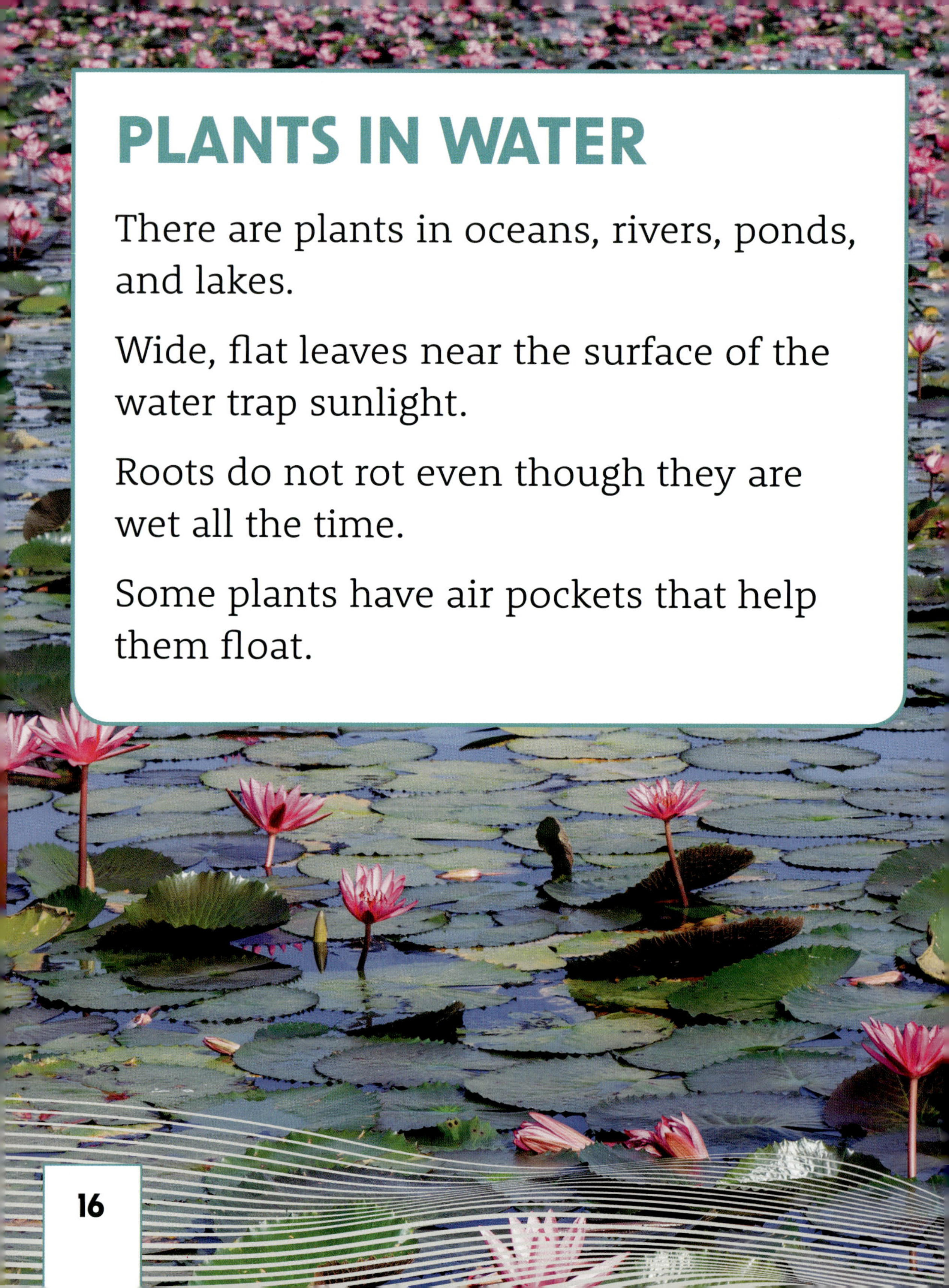

PLANTS IN WATER

There are plants in oceans, rivers, ponds, and lakes.

Wide, flat leaves near the surface of the water trap sunlight.

Roots do not rot even though they are wet all the time.

Some plants have air pockets that help them float.

FUN FACTS

The kelp plant has a part on its base that helps it stand straight in the water.

CAREER: Plant Geneticist

Plant geneticists do research to make plants better or to create new plants.

Some plants they invent are resistant to diseases.

They design plants that can live with very little water.

These scientists can make plants more **nutritious** or have new colors.

INVESTIGATE: Hydroponic Garden

Materials:

- Clean, empty two-liter bottle without the cap
- Permanent marker
- Scissors
- Water
- Old washcloth
- Coconut coir pith (or another growing medium)
- Seeds for herbs or leafy vegetables
- Aluminum foil

Procedure:

(1) Use the marker to draw a line around the bottle several inches below the neck, just under where the curve ends and the side of the bottle changes into a vertical line.

(2) Use scissors to cut the line. Flip the top piece over and place into the bottom of the bottle.

(3) Pour water into the bottom of the bottle until it almost reaches the hole.

(4) Cut the washcloth into a strip and thread it down through the hole and into the water.

(5) Wet the coco coir and use it to fill the bowl made by the top of the bottle.

(6) Plant 3 to 4 seeds in the coir.

(7) Wrap foil around the bottle, covering the sides and the bottom.

(8) Place in an area that gets as much natural sunlight as possible.

(9) Check the water to make sure it is at the correct level.

(10) As they grow, cut off the large outer leaves and enjoy eating!

THE SCIENTIFIC METHOD

- Ask a question.
- Gather information and observe.
- Make a hypothesis or guess the answer.
- Experiment and test your hypothesis, or guess.
- Analyze your test results.
- Modify your hypothesis, if necessary.
- Make a conclusion.

SCIENTIST SPOTLIGHT

Scientist Alfred Crosby and his team created a super strong adhesive called Geckskin. It was inspired by the amazing feet of geckos. A small piece can hang a television on a glass wall, but can be removed without leaving any residue. Crosby and his team have been working on creating a version that can go on more surfaces.

GLOSSARY

antifreeze (AN-tee-freez): something that lowers the freezing point of a liquid

desert (DEZ-urt): a dry area that receives little rain

environments (en-VYE-ruhn-muhntz): natural surroundings of living things, including the air, water, soil, other living things, etc.

metabolism (muh-TAB-uh-liz-uhm): the process by which food is changed into energy and chemicals in plants and animals

nutritious (noo-TRISH-uhs): healthy

opossums (uh-PAH-suhms): small mammals with a pointed nose and a long tail used to hang from tree branches

predators (PRED-uh-tuhrz): animals that hunt other animals for food

rainforest (RAYN-for-ist): a thick forest that receives a large amount of rain during the year

traits (trayts): qualities that make something different from others

venom (VEN-uhm): poison from snakes, scorpions, insects, and other animals

INDEX

AFTER READING QUESTIONS

1. Why do living things need to adapt?
2. What are behavioral adaptations?
3. Describe three adaptations that help rainforest plants survive in their environment.

About the Author

Christina Earley lives in South Florida with her husband, son, and dog. Her favorite subject in school was science. She enjoys learning the science behind the world around her, such as how roller coasters work. She loves mint chocolate chip ice cream and mermaids.

Written by: Christina Earley
Design by: Kathy Walsh
Editor: Kim Thompson

Photographs/Shutterstock: Cover & Title pg ©Kurit afshen, ©N1chEX, ©Vlad Ra27, ©Olga_C; Pg 3-19, 22, 23 ©N1chEZ; Pg 5 6, 9, 12, 17 ©Olga_C; Pg 4-5 ©Natural Earth Imagery; Pg 5 ©MyImages - Micha; Pg 6 ©MarcusVDT; Pg 7 ©Milan Zygmunt; Pg 8 ©Ken Griffiths; Pg 10 ©Maria Dryfhout; Pg 11 ©Travel Faery; Pg 12, 13 ©LHBLLC; Pg 14, 15 ©panotthorn phuhual; Pg 15 ©panotthorn phuhual; Pg 16 ©Porpla Wannobon; Pg 17 ©Dogora Sun; Pg 18 ©Ju PhotoStocker; Pg 19 ©Roman Rvachov; Pg 21 ©Paul Looyen, ©Pixel-Shot

Library of Congress PCN Data
Adaptations / Christina Earley
Life Science
ISBN 978-1-63897-492-5 (hard cover)
ISBN 978-1-63897-607-3 (paperback)
ISBN 978-1-63897-722-3 (EPUB)
ISBN 978-1-63897-837-4 (eBook)
Library of Congress Control Number: 2022930849

Printed in the United States of America.

Seahorse Publishing Company
www.seahorsepub.com

Published in the United States
Seahorse Publishing
PO Box 771325
Coral Springs, FL 33077